The "true book" series is prepared
under the direction of
Illa Podendorf
Laboratory School, University of Chicago
Ninety-eight per cent of the text is in words from
the Combined Word List for Primary Reading

the true book of

COMMUNICATION

By O. Irene Sevrey Miner
Pictures by Irene Miner and Katherine Evans

 CHILDRENS PRESS, CHICAGO

6 7 8 9 10 11 12 13 14 15 16 17 18 19 20 21 22 23 24 25   R   75 74 73 72 71 70

Library of Congress Catalog Card Number: 60-11156

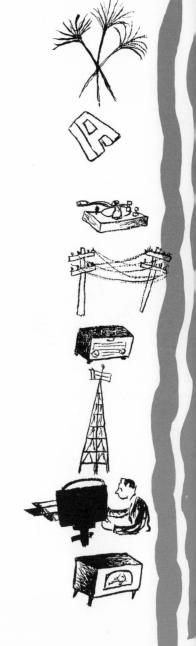

COMMUNICATION

We like to talk
with someone.
We like to listen.
We learn how others
think and feel.

The best way for us
to talk is face-to-face.
Eyes and hands can
say as much as words.
We get the message.

This is COMMUNICATION.

We cannot always
talk face-to-face.
Sometimes it is fun
to talk in only words.

Many, many things help us
send messages to each other.

NEWSPAPERS

MAGAZINES

BOOKS

LETTERS

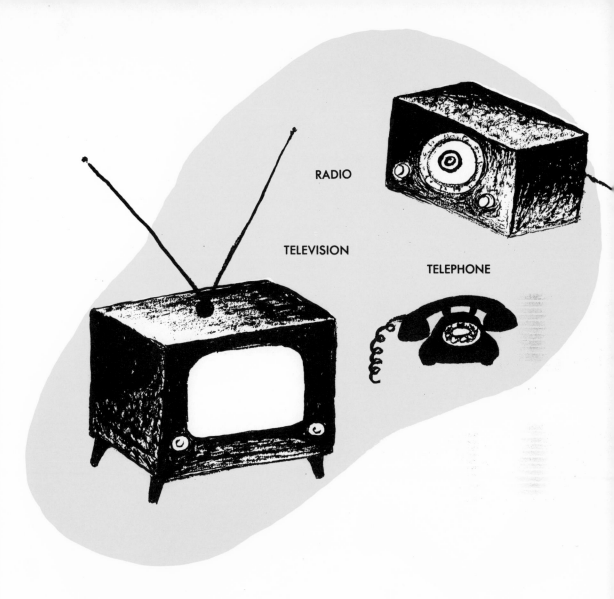

RADIO

TELEVISION

TELEPHONE

These are called
WAYS OF COMMUNICATION.

We talk with our
lips, tongues, throats.
We hear with our ears.
We see with our eyes.

Some people must learn to talk or listen or see in some other way.

SPEAKING WITH
HAND SIGNS

READING
BRAILLE

LISTENING
WITH FINGERS
ON SPEAKER'S
THROAT

We get many messages without words.

A friend nods his head, smiles or waves his hand to say HELLO.

A dog wags his tail.

We can see that rain is coming by storm clouds in the sky.

We can tell what kind of animal went by from his tracks in the sand or snow.

These things are called SIGNS.

Our ears pick up
messages that help
us to live safely.

SIGNALS

Sometimes we are too
far away to be heard.
Then we talk by SIGNALS.

SYMBOLS

Pictures and statues
are SYMBOLS.

Numbers, the alphabet
and music notes are
symbols.

Calendars, maps
and flags are symbols.

We know what symbols
mean. They become a
way of communication.

COMMUNICATION LONG AGO

Before Early Man learned to talk, he made motions and grunted. If hurt, he cried out.

If angry, he shook a club and growled.

Babies do some of these things to tell how they feel.

Maybe Man learned to talk
by hearing a bee *buzz*,
a bird *caw*,
a stick *snap*
or a fish *splash*
in water.

Some of Man's first messages told his friends where to hunt for food, and how to follow a trail.

A pile of rocks or a bent tree could say, "Go this way."

Many stones in a circle meant many buffaloes.

Cave children may have made
the first pictures in the sand.
Then their fathers began
drawing animals and men on the
walls of the caves. Some of
these pictures can be seen today.

Soon these pictures were made to tell a story.

Later they were carved on stone outside the caves, so other people could see them.

The pictures told stories about hunting and fighting and showed how people lived then.

A few people began to travel
from village to village. New
things were learned. Messages
were sent from one town to another.
Some men traveled around
telling and singing stories and news.

Kings of many countries
began sending messages by men
called "runners." Later, the
messengers traveled on horseback.
News traveled faster and faster.
Some messages were too long
to remember. So the messengers
made up new stories or news.

MESSAGES IN WRITING

Then one day a picture message was carved on a flat stone.

Stone was heavy to carry, so someone made clay tablets. They tried using blocks of wood covered with wax. But clay would break and wax would melt, so they tried other things.

Making a picture for everything was hard. So the carver began to leave out parts of the picture. Soon it became only a shape which meant a picture.

These shapes were SYMBOLS. Each shape meant one kind of sound. Years later, someone made a "letter" for each sound. This was the first alphabet.

THE PAPER PLANT

Stone and clay and wood were hard to write on and heavy to carry. People found they could make paper-like sheets from a water reed called *papyrus*. They could write on these sheets with a reed pen.

Now many messages and books were written. People learned to read.

It took time
to send a message
from one village to another by
a runner or a rider.

Sometimes, drums, shells, horns
and smoke signals were used.

Papyrus did not grow in many countries, so people began to look for other writing materials.

They found that skins of lambs and sheep could be prepared so that they could be written on. These skins were called *parchment*.

PAPER AND PRINTING

People in China watched the hornet making its nest. The hornet used dry wood. He mixed the wood with a liquid in his mouth. His jaws made it into a pulp. Then he built his nest with this pulp.

The Chinese people copied the hornet's work and made paper.

Then the Chinese people carved pictures on blocks of wood.

These blocks were painted with ink and pressed against the paper. Many sheets of paper could be "printed" with one block of wood.

Soon both words and pictures were carved on blocks of wood.

Years later, a wise printer
carved an alphabet out of
wood. These letters could
be put together to make words
and used over and over again.

Another printer used an old
wine press to push the letters
against the paper.

Later, the letters were
made out of metal.

Travelers stopped at inns which were good places to get news.

One day someone wrote the news and posted it in the street.

Another man had his news printed and sold it to the people.

A man named Samuel B. Morse had an idea. He would send messages over a wire with the help of electricity. The messages were sent in long and short clicks that stood for letters of the alphabet. The clicks are called "dots and dashes." This is the Morse Code.

. . . — — — . . .

S   O   S

If news could travel by wire over land, why not by wire under the ocean?

After many months of hard work and several tries, the great Atlantic cable was laid between America and Europe. Now news could travel across the ocean very quickly.

Later, the telephone made
a better way to communicate.

Voice sounds were sent over
a wire as electric impulses.
These were changed back to
voice sounds in the tele-
phone receiver.

Now people, miles apart,
can talk to each other.

The telephone was a wonderful invention. But a man began to think about sending messages without wires.

He built two high towers. He put an antenna on top of each tower. After a long time, he was able to send "dots and dashes" from one tower to the other. This was the first *wireless*.

Not long after the wireless came into use, a "tube" was built. It looked a little like a light bulb. The tube made it possible to hear a person's voice instead of the dot and dash.

This tube was called a radio tube. Soon all wireless was called *radio*. Now we hear news, music and plays by radio.

MOVING PICTURES

Long ago, children had a toy which looked like a drum. Several pictures, each a little different, were put around the drum. When the drum was turned fast, the pictures seemed to move.

A camera was made which could take pictures very fast. Another machine showed them so fast that they "moved." *Moving pictures!*

Now television cameras take pictures and we can see them at the same time in our living rooms on our television sets.

Ever since the cave man began to point and growl, we have been learning better ways to communicate.

We have a language which we speak and write and read. We share ideas with people far and near. Books speak to us from the past.

Other countries have other languages. The more languages we know the better we can communicate with and understand people in other parts of the world.

Je m'appelle
Jacques.

My name is
John.

Morse Code: (International)

A · —		N — ·
B — · · ·		O — — —
C — · — ·		P · — — ·
D — · ·		Q — — · —
E ·		R · — ·
F · · — ·		S · · ·
G — — ·		T —
H · · · ·		U · · —
I · ·		V · · · —
J · — — —		W · — —
K — · —		X — · · —
L · — · ·		Y — · — —
M — —		Z — — · ·
Period (.) · — · — · —		Query (?) · · — — · ·
Comma (,) — — · · — —		Error · · · · · · · ·